Necessary Words

Raymond Tong

Published 2006

Athelney
Frithgarth
Thetford Forest Park
Hockwold-cum-Wilton
Norfolk
IP26 4NQ

© Raymond Tong

British Library Cataloguing-in-Publication Data. A
catalogue record for this book is available from the
British Library.

ISBN 1–903313-05-8

DON

Author's Note

Some of these poems have previously appeared in my *Selected Poems*, published by Robert Hale Ltd and in my collection, *Returning Home*, published by the University of Salzburg Press. Some have also appeared in The Spectator, New Statesman, Encounter, Contemporary Review, Outposts Poetry Quarterly, The Gadfly, Acumen, Chapman, Lines Review, The Poet's Voice, Thumbscrew and This England.

RT

Contents

Necessary Words

'This is our country'. At last the words
were uttered: four simple words my ancestors
would have spoken clearly with passion and pride.

Hesitating, I had only muttered them,
as though the words themselves were loath to be heard,
were somehow strangely forbidden or else untrue.

I had been taught they were dangerous words,
words to be held in check, not to be used
in view of their likely effect on others.

And yet they are very necessary words:
as necessary to the English as to the Scots,
the Welsh, the Irish or the Japanese.

Feeding the Pigeons

I wonder if I am only imagining
that many of the pigeons in this square
are lame, that wherever I go more and more
trees seem to be dying, that the annual miracle
of butterflies has become much less apparent.

I wonder if I am only imagining
that while more people concern themselves
with problems of poverty in distant lands
they often seem to have less and less
love remaining for those nearest to them.

I wonder if I am only imagining
that centuries of pride are slowly draining
from this city, daily leaving more rubbish
in the streets, more graffiti on the walls
and more violent behaviour than ever before.

I wonder if I am only imagining
that more and more people talk to themselves
as though pondering some terrible dilemma,
the young often angry and aggressive,
the old quieter yet clearly troubled.

In a Strange Land

This is the land where the indigenous people
often appear uneasy when writing
or talking about their own nationality;
where they are often diffident, even embarrassed,
when asked about their patriotic feelings,
about their cultural identity or their nation's
resplendent history.

This is the land of the gently manipulated,
where the majority silently accept the erosion
of national beliefs and values; where native
tolerance and good nature are taken for granted
and constantly abused; where all too often
unjustified guilt takes the place
of justified pride.

My Home

"My home
is your inn."
In this manner a wise
and civilised person
welcomes a visitor.

"My home
is your home."
Thus speaks a fool
who deserves the disasters
about to happen.

The Arbiters

Here there are no whips raised in anger,
no thought-criminals or thought-police,
only the feeling of being manipulated.

Here the blandly smiling arbiters decide
how to present the awkward and unacceptable,
what should be disclosed and what withheld.

Most of the media, unlike a Ministry
of Love, does not persuade us what to think,
but much more subtly, what not to think.

Seeking to help us find enlightened answers
they make omission an equalising virtue,
obscuring every subject deemed taboo.

Observing the English

I have been observing the English.
When it is hot their behaviour
is often very strange indeed.
When it is cold their behaviour
is often equally peculiar.
And when it is neither they still
tend to behave very oddly.

While usually the Scots are Scottish,
the Irish are Irish, the Welsh are Welsh,
the English are very seldom English.
Generally the English are British,
a word encompassing the whole
island and possibly much less
evocative of patriotic emotion.

No wonder they appear to be devious.
Having helped many countries
to arrive at nationhood and having
long emphasised for others
the importance of national identity
they seem largely unconcerned
about their own identity.

They are certainly proud of their
patience and tolerance. But to a visitor
from a land with a less fortunate history
and a less comfortable present
their tolerance may often seem
complacency and patience a way
of avoiding difficult decisions.

To a Hostel Warden

You complain, Reverend Sir,
that the young Arabs living in your hostel
sit every afternoon undressing
every girl who passes through the lounge
and that the girls do not like it.

For one who is well travelled
and obviously so understanding,
I am surprised, Reverend Sir,
that you are so insensitive
to the problems of these young Arabs.
Surely you must know that they would
not behave like that in their own countries.

You must surely be aware
that they come from countries
where some women still wear veils,
where death by stoning is still
a possible penalty for adultery,
where even in universities
the sexes do not mix freely.

If you had grown up as they have
and then had the good fortune
to come to this wonderful land,
the Land of the Free and Easy,
where there is no moral reason
why anybody should not do anything,
where ass-tight trousers prevail,
where sex is everywhere
and often starts quite early,
you too, Reverend Sir,
would happily undress the girls,
even on a Sunday.

Television Interviewer

With his carefully prepared questions
in front of him he slowly raises his head
and smiles coldly into millions of homes.

Not being sure of what to expect
the public figure he will interview
patiently watches him without expression.

After two or three initial questions
it is clear the interviewer has little respect
for eminence and outstanding achievement.

As one barbed question follows another
the public figure is visibly angry
that he has to endure such interrogation.

Yet although increasingly tense he remains
very controlled and of course the interviewer
rarely exceeds the limits of his script.

With a confidential smirk the interview
at last arrives at its well-manoeuvred end,
doubtless much to the relief of the public figure.

It is all in the sacred cause of entertainment.
Many viewers enjoy the discomfiture
produced by the skilful probing of the interviewer.

But many sympathise with the public figure.
It is never pleasant to see the use of power
combined with minimal responsibility.

A few perhaps look forward to the day
when a raw nerve will reach a breaking-point
and an overpatient victim will rebel.

Then quickly the smirk will disappear.
Hopefully the interviewer will be knocked cold
or awarded a well deserved black eye.

Cinquains

Equity Decision

Sorry,
darling, any
person applying for
the role of Cromwell must be white
and male.

For Sale

Look, man,
these people take
no pride in anything
at all. You can even buy their
churches.

Black Poetry

I'd scorn
all poetry
labelled 'white'. Therefore why
should I read poetry described
as 'black'?

Caucasian

M'lud,
I'm sure they were
Caucasian. I saw
quite clearly. They all had snow on
their boots!

Not For Them

Never
could disaster
like that happen to them.
They were right. It happened to their
children.

Returning Home

recalling a conversation
with an African politician

No, sir, I do not dispute your point.
This is black man's country
and I do not belong here.
No matter how hard I work
these mountains, plains and forests
can never be my country.
The history of this land,
no matter how much interest
I have taken in it, can never
be the history of my land.
I have served this country well,
but I have only been selling
my labour, the few talents I have.
No, sir, there is nothing wrong in that.
I would not want it otherwise.

Yes, sir, I agree with you.
I will live in my own country,
the country where I belong.
I will return to the landscape
I have always carried with me:
to the orchards and farmyards,
the patchwork of green fields and hills.
I will go back to the history
revealed in ancient cathedrals and castles.
I will ponder on the gaunt relics
of those dark satanic mills
which made possible a new age,
the vision of a new Jerusalem.
Yes, sir, you have your country
and I have mine.

Legacy for Africa

Every demand was gradually conceded,
and always in the end, sooner rather
than later, independence was formally
presented with a bold flourish of trumpets.

When the trumpets ceased frustration
remained. They were left a legacy
of liberal thinking that had little to do
with the kind of freedom they were seeking.

And when it was time to enjoy their freedom,
to wield their power and bask in glory,
unfriendly foreigners spoke of corruption
and branded their leadership undemocratic.

A Commonwealth
Conference Photograph

This African potentate basks in glory,
prepared to use any means whatever
to retain his role as president for life.

This smiling little Asian demagogue,
despite his cultured liberal platitudes,
runs his police-state most efficiently.

Yet both are less politically vicious than many
of the others. At least a half of those present
come from countries far from democratic.

Indeed this nebulous, unrelated assembly
of states, often with antithetical interests,
has clearly very little to recommend it.

It seems most likely that it still survives
largely due to a self-deceiving lethargy,
a long meaningless imperial hangover.

St John and St Anselm

Grinning derisively from the twin towers
of the Church of St John and St Anselm
the gargoyles mockingly survey
the empty cans, the paper and discarded cartons,
the battered headstones and neglected graves.

A few years ago St John
and St Anselm, like the nearby
Mount of Olives, still remained a church.
Now it is used by the youthful unemployed
who take part in activities arranged
by Arts Opportunities Limited,
while the Mount of Olives is a Fitness Centre,
where unconcerned with spiritual longing
the faithful seek only the health of the body.

Doubtless St John, a shadowy mystic,
should he ever come this far north,
would gaze sadly at 'our beloved father'
beneath a broken cross, at 'dear mother'
pathetically askew in the long grass.
Yet absorbed by ineffable divinity,

having long ago witnessed the light
shining in the uncomprehending darkness,
he might be consoled that the building
is put to a seemingly useful purpose.
Quickly departing he might murmour:
'I have seen this happen before.
Soon there will be a new beginning.'

But surely Anselm, stubborn Norman saint,
reluctant archbishop to an evil king,
would react in a manner less quiescent.
Loving the English as he loved his Church,
having spent much of his life struggling
successfully against the power of the State,
he would turn away in obvious anguish.
Then oblivious of the traffic he would go
striding instinctively towards the Cathedral,
shouting angrily through his tears:
'My people, has it come to this?
Have you forgotten who you are?
Do you no longer care?'

Triolet for St John's

They have taken away great-grandfather's bones
to make an office parking space.
Having removed the old tombstones
they have taken away great-grandfather's bones.
With desks, computers and telephones
St John's will become a thriving place.
They have taken away great-grandfather's bones
to make an office parking space.

On Reading 'How to be a Brit'

The clever Mr Mikes tells us how
anyone can learn to be a Brit.
Perhaps the time has come to tell us now
how the British into Hungary can fit.

An Anglican Bishop

This Church of England bishop knows the way
to make his many doubts a source of praise.
Promoting every creed and each new craze,
he leads his flock where they were wont to stray.

A Sociologist

Your concern to preserve identities
of immigrants suggests a man who cares.
And yet, Professor, not a single word
about the natives slowly losing theirs.

Televised Protest

A young woman sobs bitterly
into relentless television cameras
and angrily refuses to move away,
frantically clinging to the trunk of a tree
on a wintry Somerset hillside.

Although sympathising with her good intentions
most viewers may feel she is over-reacting.
At a time when so much that we value
seems in danger of extinction her protest
may appear pathetic and rather foolish.

After all they are only badgers
and they are being gassed officially
on the recommendation of a government scientist.
It appears that one out of six may be
tubercular and therefore dangerous to cattle.

Yet there could easily have been badgers
on that hill for many centuries.
Unless attacked by their only enemy,
from generation to generation badgers
have no need to wander far from the birthplace.

Coming from the village in the valley
the young woman has probably known
of the badgers' presence since early childhood.
That hillside may once have been
entwined in fantasy, a place of wonder.

Perhaps she is lamenting not only the shy
stay-at-home creatures lying dead
in their burrows, but those areas of innocence,
the patches of wilderness, that gradually grow
more scarce as pressures multiply.

Other Eden

No longer such a happy breed,
and soon perhaps no breed at all,
they drift upon the tide of history,
little concerned with who they are
or where they are going.

                    No longer
secured from invasion by their moat,
increasingly aware of growing pressures,
they obscure the dilemmas that threaten
to engulf them by asserting the virtues
of patience and tolerance.

                    No longer
to be envied, their beliefs and values
constantly eroded, steadily
retreating with unfailing compromise,
they have ceased to hear the authentic cadence
of their essential being. Lacking any
unifying vision, they are slowly
falling away into everywhere
and nowhere.

In Another's Place

As the train left Waterbeach I glanced
at the book the Japanese next to me
was reading. Perhaps I expected a book on Zen
or maybe a guide to Ely Cathedral.
What I saw was a technical study
of recent developments in local agriculture.

Of course I soon realised that I had put
myself in his place. If I were travelling
by train in Japan I would probably be reading
a guide to whatever I intended to visit
or perhaps a book on some aspect of Zen,
not a study of local agriculture.

It is easy to put oneself in another's place
and so difficult to achieve understanding,
especially for people with a different culture
and history, different values and aspirations.
Even with one's compatriots understanding
each other is not always easy.

Come to think of it, if we had been
in Japan and he had observed me studying
local agriculture he might have taken
me for an imperialist dreaming of future dominion.
And who knows, perhaps that Japanese
was dreaming of something rather similar.

The Great Storm
16 October 1987

Shakespeare or Milton would have seen the hand
of God in that great storm. They would have said
that all the houses damaged, the ancient trees
uprooted, were a sign of God's anger,
a warning to a sadly erring people.

We in our age, aware of the vagrant behaviour
of isobars, mock our own incompetence.
And yet our certainty is briefly shattered,
recalling our vast vulnerability,
our endless, delicate compromise with nature.

Stamp Issues

When I first began collecting stamps
my magpie instincts were always attracted
by the large, brightly coloured colonials
with exotic names like the Congo and Togo.

I was very scornful of British issues,
feeling my country should do better
than those small, mono-coloured stamps
decorated only with the king's head.

When I asked my father why they were
so dull and unimpressive he told me
it was because a secure and powerful country
has no need of large, resplendent stamps.

He said a weak, yet aspiring country
will often take every opportunity
of attracting attention, rather like a cockerel
puffing himself out and loudly crowing.

Fifty years later, buying the latest
special issue of large, brightly coloured
British stamps, I feel strangely troubled,
recalling my father's simple explanation.

I Let It Happen

I let it happen
- me and a few million others.
Although I was aware
of the motives involved
and knew what was intended
I did nothing to prevent it.
I uttered not a word of protest,
but turned my back on what I saw
and went off muttering to myself
that one only lives once,
that I had a living to earn,
and besides there was nothing
I could do about it.

Nobody was ever consulted.
Nobody asked me or a few million
others if we wanted it to happen.
It was foisted upon us,
gradually, almost imperceptibly,
until the point was reached
when there seemed no going back.
And being the sort of people we are
we pretended not to notice.
If anybody had asked us
we would probably have said
it was really not so bad,
we were getting used to it.

Portrait

The iron bangle on his wrist
when worn by a Sikh is called a kara.
With long hair, short pants,
a comb and a dagger it indicates
a member of the Sikh religion.
While sensing its original
purpose, he is not concerned
with any religious symbolism.
Like those shining swastikas,
the shirt made from a Union Jack,
the red and blue Mohican plume
upon his shaven head, the kara
is merely an item in his regalia
of rebellion, a violent decoration,
a silent revolt against being
a part of everything and nothing,
a sturdy companion to the studs
upon his boots and leather jacket.

Bosworth - 1485

'Henry Tudor, I challenge you
to single combat.' Richard's words
echoed across Bosworth Field.

Henry Tudor did not reply,
and so the King's herald repeated
the challenge three more times.

But still Henry did not reply.
Aware of Lord Stanley's treacherous
manoeuvres, he smiled contemptuously.

And thus it passed that turbulent age
of proud dedication, its spirit
sublimely embodied in Gothic cathedrals.

On the Statue of Oliver Cromwell at Westminster

With his left hand holding the Bible
and with his right hand resting on
his unsheathed sword, this most English
of all Englishmen stands for ever steadfast
and unvanquished. As he sternly surveys
the passers-by, his commanding presence
recalls the puritan lover of wine and music,
the practical mystic, the inspired leader,
devotedly served by Milton and Marvell.
It recalls the stubborn patriot firmly
rooted in his fertile fenland acres,
reluctantly accepting his destiny,
becoming the dominant figure of his age.
It recalls a triumph of Englishness; a man
intuitively just and reasonable,
yet relentless in defending liberty
of conscience, parliamentary institutions
and his nation's interests.

Milton: 1660

The voice of one crying in every vein,
unable to suppress his growing rage,
groping ancestral caverns of the brain,
gazing through darkness at the empty page.

Without regeneration of the mind
always the Cause would be frustrated: greed
and self-interest would for ever find
the means to thwart even the noblest creed.

Yet he would come to terms with their defeat,
slowly accepting they had left the field.
Although henceforth dissent would be discreet,
like fallen Satan he would never yield.

His epic verse would take a lofty stance,
showing that what was lost could be regained.
For Samson there would be a second chance
and those he wished to reach would understand.

Gulls

From green turf on the white cliffs,
so lately a symbol of our love,
see how the gulls wheel
and strategically glide,
soar through swirling currents of air,
screaming in protest
as the storm draws near,
strenuously ride the rising wind, then fall
steeply in aerial combat above
the foaming and invading tide.

The Third World

The Third World
is not a geographical location.
It is not defined by colour or creed.
It does not consist only of dark-skinned people
submerged by the corruption and chaos
of some tropical tyranny.

The Third World
is a mindless state of acceptance,
the spiritual darkness all around us,
whether in Africa or Asia,
in London, Paris, New York
or your own home town.

It exists wherever people have lost
or never had a sense of striving,
where inwardly gazing they wait
for the fruit to fall from the tree,
for the gods to reveal a benevolence
that is always predictably absent.

After the Explosion

(i)
For over a week after the explosion
a vast cloud of dense brown smoke
drifted above the northern counties of England,
seeming to envelop every town and village
north of York almost to the Scottish border.
As the nature of the disaster became evident,
the Government placed two protective barriers
of troops across the country from Blackpool
to Scarborough and from Carlisle to Berwick.
This ensured that nobody ventured
into the Zone and, owing to the likelihood
of contagion, that nobody came out.

(ii)
Incredible as it now may seem, owing
to the problems experienced by the troops
in preventing hordes of frightened people
from breaking through their protective cordons,
two weeks elapsed before the Special
Emergency Force entered the stricken region.
When they were finally able to do so
they found that much of the countryside
had assumed a strangely lunar aspect.
A substance rather like grey snow
had settled evenly upon the landscape,
providing a sombre and eerie back-cloth
for the long queues of desperate survivors
slowly moving along the main roads.

Refusal to Accept

Though the disease was far advanced
he refused to accept its existence.

That such a comfortable life
could come to an end seemed quite absurd.

When warned of the need for surgery
he appeared surprised and failed to respond.

Thus no cure was possible.
The consequent decline was slow and agonising.

Figures on a Desolate Landscape

Whispering their doom these figures pause
upon this ruined landscape of their fear,
no longer caring that the end draws near,
nor seeking to escape or find the cause
of such disaster.

        Look! behind them leer
the Furies, shrieking how their God has died,
how they themselves are now the crucified,
poor clay dissolving in the cosmic sneer
of blindest Fate.

        But yet they do not hear,
these figures, how the Furies' shrieks deride
their end, for soon each staggers and then falls,
clutching each ragged dream that once was dear,
lost in the deathless beauty of the void,
the desolation of these darkening hills.

The Day of Reckoning

And so the day of reckoning had come.
Nearly everything he had believed in,
or had worked for, would be swept away.

His first reaction was to cut his losses,
to stop speculating about the future
and quietly depart for another country.

It was no good pretending. Earth could show
many cities more fair. Jerusalem
would not be built in this overcrowded island.

Yet where would he go? Wherever he went
there would be the same lack of meaning,
the same anguish and aimless posturing.

In the end he would stay. Accepting
once more the need to compromise
he would assist the bad against the worse.

A School Photograph

It hangs forsaken on a store-room wall:
the Football First Eleven in thirty-nine.
How proud I was to play at last for the School,
slender perhaps but with the will to shine.

Six of that smiling team were killed in the War.
They all accepted what seemed an obvious truth:
it was their country they were fighting for,
the gentle English landscape of their youth.

Today this photograph brings only sadness.
Seeing those faces almost moves me to tears.
I recall that angry age of far-flung madness,
our political weakness in preceding years.

And thinking of all that has happened since then,
how little of what they fought for still survives,
it seems my friends were sacrificed in vain,
the outcome not worth the loss of their young lives.

Problems

Suddenly problems began to multiply.
At home, in shops and pubs, on television,
everybody discussed the latest problems.

We largely function now in terms of problems.
Each day provides the problems to be solved.
When they do not exist we soon invent them.

And naturally people themselves are problems.
Children, the young, the middle-aged, the old:
all are problems, often insoluble problems.

The Pond

Often I have dreamed about the pond,
an English pond, mysteriously deep
at one end. Usually there are newts
and tadpoles, and even dragon-flies.

Sometimes it becomes wider and murkier,
no longer surrounded by reeds and bushes,
but by familiar jungle, huge boulders
and high trees. It is then I see the lions.

At least I used to. Now visions of Africa
will cease to mingle with my early years.
For yesterday I ventured past the dream,
exploring the source of so much wonder.

There was no trace of my boyhood pond,
no water for tadpoles and newts,
no reeds and bushes for dragon-flies,
only a dreary road of identical houses.

An English Prayer

Lord, grant to the people of England
the grace to remember who they are.
Help them to resist the gradual falling
away into everywhere and nowhere
and to heed again the authentic cadence
of their essential being.

Give them the will to rouse themselves
once more from long indifference.
Strengthen, O Lord, their purpose and pride,
that they may resolve in the years ahead
never to forsake that inner self,
the precious core of history.

Words that Rankle

Words can rankle for many years,
creating a barrier none can rend:
received with anger or with tears
they sometimes linger to the end.

Usually the words that fester
are not vitriolic or obscene,
not the words of a spiteful jester,
vicious and most cruelly mean.

Often the words that crucify
are quietly uttered with a smile:
unforgivable the subtle lie,
the venom masked by gentle guile.

But most unforgivable of all
are the words, often simple and few,
whose barbs pierce an Achilles' heel
and wound the deepest, being true.

Some other Athelney titles

The English Dragon
T.P. Bragg

This is an original and well-told tale about loss of innocence and a search for identity. The narrative gives the flavour of modern England and a culture obsessed with image and dogma. A comparison is made between a rural, traditional community and an often violent urban society. Subjects dealt with include the treatment and housing of asylum-seekers in rural areas.

£5-95 A5 ISBN 1-903313-02-3 232 pages

Views from the English Community
Edited by Tony Linsell

A collection of 44 essays and poems written by 15 members of the English community. Topics covered include: The origins and early history of the English; English folksong and music; William Cobbett - English radical; The onslaught on English identity and the English way-of-life; Multiculturalism - a deeply flawed dogma?; Short stories about contemporary England; The case for an English parliament; Modern English nationalism.

£14-95 ISBN 1-898281-36-X 254 x 170mm / 10 x 6¾ inches hardcover 256 pages

The Deculturalisation of the English People
The Rev. John Lovejoy

In Australia the author witnessed the sad fate of Aborigines who have had their culture and communal life shattered. On his return to England, he saw the English facing a similar process of deculturalisation but lacking the will to resist or reverse it.

The young have no sense of who they are or where they are from. Deculturalisation is revealed in the inability of many, and especially the young, to be able to answer the questions, Who am I? What do I believe? Where do I belong? Who am I loyal to?

Everywhere we see the loss of communal values and perceptions. John Lovejoy gives reasons for the deculturalisation of the English and points to the remedy.

£4-95 A5 ISBN 1-903313-00-7 80 pages

An English Nationalism
Tony Linsell

In this handbook of modern nationalism the author starts by investigating the origins of the English and England. This is followed by an exploration of what constitutes a nation – is it merely a collection of individuals living together in a state or is it a group of people who share a common history, ancestry, way-of-life, and communal identity?

"Our political institutions deny us meaningful choice. A democratic system should aim to give us the ability to govern ourselves, which includes the management of our economy, culture, and physical environment. Yet the trend in modern politics is to deny us this control. Instead, we are increasingly in the thrall of the unelected and unaccountable."

£16-90 248 x 170mm ISBN 1-903313-01-5 430 pages

Some other titles from Anglo-Saxon Books

An Introduction to the Old English Language and its Literature
Stephen Pollington

The purpose of this general introduction to Old English is not to deal with the teaching of Old English but to dispel some misconceptions about the language and to give an outline of its structure and its literature. Some basic knowledge about the origins of the English language and its early literature is essential to an understanding of the early period of English history and the present form of the language. This revised and expanded edition provides a useful guide for those contemplating embarking on a linguistic journey.

£4.95 A5 ISBN 1–898281–06–8 64 pages

First Steps in Old English
An easy to follow language course for the beginner
Stephen Pollington

A complete and easy to use Old English language course that contains all the exercises and texts needed to learn Old English. This course has been designed to be of help to a wide range of students, from those who are teaching themselves at home, to undergraduates who are learning Old English as part of their English degree course. The author is aware that some individuals have difficulty with grammar. To help overcome this and other difficulties, he has adopted a step-by-step approach that enables students of differing abilities to advance at their own pace. The course includes practice and translation exercises.

There is a glossary of the words used in the course, and 16 Old English texts, including the Battle of Brunanburh and Battle of Maldon.

£16-95 ISBN 1–898281–19–X 248 x 173mm / 10 x 6½ inches 256 pages

Ærgeweorc: Old English Verse and Prose read by Stephen Pollington

This audiotape cassette can be used in conjunction with *First Steps in Old English* or just listened to for the sheer pleasure of hearing Old English spoken well.
Tracks: 1. Deor. 2. Beowulf – The Funeral of Scyld Scefing. 3. Engla Tocyme (The Arrival of the English). 4. Ines Domas. Two Extracts from the Laws of King Ine. 5. Deniga Hergung (The Danes' Harrying) Anglo-Saxon Chronicle Entry AD997. 6. Durham 7. The Ordeal (Be ðon ðe ordales weddigaþ) 8. Wið Dweorh (Against a Dwarf) 9. Wið Wennum (Against Wens) 10. Wið Wæterælfadle (Against Waterelf Sickness) 11. The Nine Herbs Charm 12. Læcedomas (Leechdoms) 13. Beowulf's Greeting 14. The Battle of Brunanburh 15. Blacmon – by Adrian Pilgrim.

£7.50 ISBN 1–898281–20–3 C40 audiotape Old English transcript supplied with tape.

Wordcraft Concise English/Old English Dictionary and Thesaurus
Stephen Pollington

Wordcraft provides Old English equivalents to the commoner modern words in both dictionary and thesaurus formats. The Thesaurus presents vocabulary relevant to a wide range of individual topics in alphabetical lists, thus making it easily accessible to those with specific areas of interest. Each thematic listing is encoded for cross-reference from the Dictionary.

The two sections will be of invaluable assistance to students of the language, as well as those with either a general or a specific interest in the Anglo-Saxon period.

£9.95 ISBN 1–898281–02–5 A5 256 pages

Looking for the Lost Gods of England
Kathleen Herbert

Kathleen Herbert sifts through the royal genealogies, charms, verse and other sources to find clues to the names and attributes of the Gods and Goddesses of the early English. The earliest account of English heathen practices reveals that they worshipped the Earth Mother and called her Nerthus. The tales, beliefs and traditions of that time are still with us and able to stir our minds and imaginations.

£4.95   ISBN 1–898281–04–1   A5   64 pages

Anglo-Saxon Food & Drink
Production, Processing, Distribution, and Consumption
Ann Hagen

Food production for home consumption was the basis of economic activity throughout the Anglo-Saxon period. Used as payment and a medium of trade, food was the basis of the Anglo-Saxons' system of finance and administration.

Information from various sources has been brought together in order to build up a picture of how food was grown, conserved, distributed, prepared and eaten during the period from the beginning of the 5th century to the 11th century. Many people will find it fascinating for the views it gives of an important aspect of Anglo-Saxon life and culture. In addition to Anglo-Saxon England the Celtic west of Britain is also covered.

This edition combines earlier titles – *A Handbook of Anglo-Saxon Food* and *A Second Handbook of Anglo-Saxon Food & Drink*.

Extensive index.

£25   10" x 7" (250 x 175mm)   ISBN 1–898281–41-6   Hardback 512pp

Anglo-Saxon Riddles
Translated by John Porter

This is a book full of ingenious characters who speak their names in riddles. Here you will meet a one-eyed garlic seller, a bookworm, an iceberg, an oyster, the sun and moon and a host of others from the everyday life and imagination of the Anglo-Saxons.

John Porter's sparkling translations retain all the vigour and subtly of the original Old English poems, transporting us back over a thousand years to the roots of our language and literature.

Contains all 95 riddles of the Exeter Book in Old English with Modern English translations.

£4.95   ISBN 1–898281–32–7   A5   112 pages

An Introduction to Early English Law
Bill Griffiths

Much of Anglo-Saxon life followed a traditional pattern, of custom, and of dependence on kin-groups for land, support and security. The Viking incursions of the ninth century and the re-conquest of the north that followed both disturbed this pattern and led to a new emphasis on centralised power and law, with royal and ecclesiastical officials prominent as arbitrators and settlers of disputes.

The diversity and development of early English law is sampled here by selecting several law-codes to be read in translation – that of Ethelbert of Kent, being the first to be issued in England, Alfred the Great's, the most clearly thought-out of all, and short codes from the reigns of Edmund and Ethelred the Unready.

£4.95   ISBN 1–898281–14–9   A5   96 pages

Peace-Weavers and Shield-Maidens: Women in Early English Society
Kathleen Herbert

The recorded history of the English people did not start in 1066 as popularly believed but one thousand years earlier. The Roman historian Cornelius Tacitus noted in *Germania*, published in the year 98, that the English (Latin *Anglii*), who lived in the southern part of the Jutland peninsula, were members of an alliance of Goddess-worshippers. The author has taken that as an appropriate opening to an account of the earliest Englishwomen, the part they played in the making of England, what they did in peace and war, the impressions they left in Britain and on the continent, how they were recorded in the chronicles, how they come alive in heroic verse and jokes.

£4.95   ISBN 1–898281–11–4   A5   64 pages

Dark Age Naval Power
A Reassessment of Frankish and Anglo-Saxon Seafaring Activity
John Haywood

In the first edition of this work, published in 1991, John Haywood argued that the capabilities of the pre-Viking Germanic seafarers had been greatly underestimated. Since that time, his reassessment of Frankish and Anglo-Saxon shipbuilding and seafaring has been widely praised and accepted.

'The book remains a historical study of the first order. It is required reading for our seminar on medieval seafaring at Texas A & M University and is essential reading for anyone interested in the subject.'   F. H. Van Doorninck, *The American Neptune* (1994)

'The author has done a fine job, and his clear and strongly put theories will hopefully further the discussion of this important part of European history.'
          Arne Emil Christensen, *The International Journal of Nautical Archaeology* (1992)

In this second edition, some sections of the book have been revised and updated to include information gained from excavations and sea trials with sailing replicas of early ships. The new evidence supports the author's argument that early Germanic shipbuilding and seafaring skills were far more advanced than previously thought. It also supports the view that Viking ships and seaborne activities were not as revolutionary as is commonly believed.

5 maps & 18 illustrations

£16.95 ISBN 1–898281–43-2   approx. 10" x 7" (250 x 175mm) 224 pp

The English Warrior from earliest times to 1066
Stephen Pollington

"An under-the-skin study of the role, rights, duties, psyche and rituals of the Anglo-Saxon warrior. The author combines original translations from Norse and Old English primary sources with archaeological and linguistic evidence for an in-depth look at the warrior, his weapons, tactics and logistics.

A very refreshing, innovative and well-written piece of scholarship that illuminates a neglected period of English history"

Time Team Booklists - Channel 4 Television

This is not intended to be a bald listing of the battles and campaigns from the Anglo-Saxon Chronicle and other sources, but rather it is an attempt to get below the surface of Anglo-Saxon warriorhood and to investigate the rites, social attitudes, mentality and mythology of the warfare of those times.

Revised Edition
An already highly acclaimed book has been made even better by the inclusion of additional information and illustrations.

£16.95   ISBN 1–898281–42-4   10" x 7" (250 x 175mm)   +50 illustrations   288 pages

English Martial Arts
Terry Brown

Sixteenth century English martial artists had their own governing body, the Company of Maisters, which taught and practised a fighting system that ranks as high in terms of effectiveness and pedigree as any in the world.

Experienced martial artists, irrespective of the style they practice, will recognise that the techniques and methods of this system are based on principles that are as valid as those that underlie the system that they practice.

Experienced martial artists, irrespective of the style they practice, will recognise that the techniques and methods of this system are based on principles that are as valid as those that underlie the system that they themselves practice.

I found the historical accounts of these martial artists amazing...If you have any interest in martial arts at all, be it weapons or empty hand combat, then this book is a must, not only for the practical depiction of the techniques but for the in-depth historical facts surrounding our own island's martial discipline.

Pat O'Malley, Martial Arts Illustrated, U.K.

It is very well done, with very valuable material. It is a welcomed study, smoothly written.

John Clements, Historical Armed Combat Association U.S.A.

I highly recommend this book; I particularly like the fighting terminology he has researched, which provides documented period names (in English, no less) for many of the fighting stances and guards we in the SCA currently use under a bewildering number of different names. ...Techniques from English Martial Arts can also provide the basis for a very good training program for newer fighters, or for experienced fighters learning a new weapon style.

Michael Lacy, Flame Journal, (Society for Creative Anachronisms)

£16.95   ISBN 1–898281–29-7   10" x 7" (250 x 175mm)   220 photographs   240 pages

Sixty Saxon Saints
Alan Smith

A useful concise guide which contains biographical details of most of the better known English saints and a calendar of their feast days. The purpose of this booklet is to see some justice done to the English saints of the Anglo-Saxon period who took with them from the secular into the religious life the native English ideals of loyalty to one's Lord and, if necessary, sacrificial service to his cause.

£3.50   ISBN 1–898281–07–6   A5 booklet with stiff card cover   48 pages

The Hallowing of England
A guide to the saints of Old England and their places of pilgrimage
Father Andrew Phillips

In the Old English period we can count over 300 saints, yet today their names and exploits are largely unknown. They are part of a forgotten England which, though it lies deep in the past, is an important part of our national and spiritual history.

An alphabetical list of 260 saints cross referenced to an alphabetical list of over 300 places with which the saints are associated; brief biographical details of 22 patriarchs of the English Church; a calendar of saint's feast days.

£4.95   ISBN 1–898281–08–4   A5   96 pages

The Battle of Maldon
Text and Translation
Translated and edited by Bill Griffiths

The Battle of Maldon was fought between the men of Essex and the Vikings in AD 991. The action was captured in an Anglo-Saxon poem whose vividness and heroic spirit has fascinated readers and scholars for generations. *The Battle of Maldon* includes the source text; edited text; parallel literal translation; verse translation; notes on pronunciation; review of 103 books and articles. This new edition (the fourth) includes notes on Old English verse.

£4.95   ISBN 0–9516209–0–8   A5   96 pages

Note: *The Battle of Maldon* and *Beowulf* have been produced with edited Old English texts and parallel literal modern English translations which will be of help to those learning Old English.

Beowulf: Text and Translation
Translated by John Porter

The verse in which the story unfolds is, by common consent, the finest writing surviving in Old English, a text which all students of the language and many general readers will want to tackle in the original form. To aid understanding of the Old English, a literal word-by-word translation is printed opposite the edited text and provides a practical key to this Anglo-Saxon masterpiece. The literal translation is very helpful for those learning or practicing Old English, however, it is not a good way to read the story. For that, we recommend *Beowulf* by Kevin Crossley-Holland – published by Penguin.

£8.95   ISBN 0–9516209–2–4   A5   192 pages

Alfred's Metres of Boethius
Edited by Bill Griffiths

In this new edition of the Old English *Metres of Boethius*, clarity of text, informative notes and a helpful glossary have been a priority, for this is one of the most approachable of Old English verse texts, lucid and delightful; its relative neglect by specialists will mean this text will come as a new experience to many practised students of the language; while its clear, expositional verse style makes it an ideal starting point for all amateurs of the period.

In these poems, King Alfred re-built the Latin verses from Boethius' *De Consolatione Philosophiae* ("On the Consolation of Philosophy") into new alliterative poems, via an Old English prose intermediary. The text is in effect a compendium of late classical science and philosophy, tackling serious issues like the working of the universe, the nature of the soul, the morality of power – but presented in so clear and lively a manner as to make it as challenging today as it was in those surprisingly UN-Dark Ages. The text is in Old English without Modern English translation

£14.95   ISBN 1–898281–03–3   250 x 175mm / 10 x 7inches   208 pages

Aspects of Anglo-Saxon Magic
Bill Griffiths

Magic is something special, something unauthorised; an alternative perhaps; even a deliberate cultivation of dark, evil powers. But for the Anglo-Saxon age, the neat division between mainstream and occult, rational and superstitious, Christian and pagan is not always easy to discern. To maintain its authority (or its monopoly?) the Church drew a formal line and outlawed a range of dubious practices (like divination, spells, folk healing) while at the same time conducting very similar rituals itself, and may even have adapted legends of elves to serve in a Christian explanation of disease as a battle between good and evil, between Church and demons; in other cases powerful ancestors came to serve as saints.

In pursuit of a better understanding of Anglo-Saxon magic, a wide range of topics and texts are examined in this book, challenging (constructively, it is hoped) our stereotyped images of the past and its beliefs.

Texts are printed in their original language (e.g. Old English, Icelandic, Latin) with New English translations. Contents include:– twenty charms; the English, Icelandic and Norwegian rune poems; texts on dreams, weather signs, unlucky days, the solar system; and much more.

£16.95   ISBN 1–898281–15–7   10" x 7" (250 x 175mm)   hardback   256 pages

Anglo-Saxon Runes
John M. Kemble

Kemble's essay *On Anglo-Saxon Runes* first appeared in the journal *Archaeologia* for 1840; it draws on the work of Wilhelm Grimm, but breaks new ground for Anglo-Saxon studies in his survey of the Ruthwell Cross and the Cynewulf poems. It is an expression both of his own indomitable spirit and of the fascination and mystery of the Runes themselves, making it an attractive introduction to the topic.

For this edition new notes have been supplied, which include translations of Latin and Old English material quoted in the text, to make this key work in the study of runes more accessible to the general reader.

£4.95 ISBN 0–9516209–1–6 A5 80 pages

The Mead-Hall
The feasting tradition in Anglo-Saxon England
Stephen Pollington

This new study takes a broad look at the subject of halls and feasting in Anglo-Saxon England. The idea of the communal meal was very important among nobles and yeomen, warriors, farmers churchmen and laity. One of the aims of the book is to show that there was not just one 'feast' but two main types: the informal social occasion *gebeorscipe* and the formal, ritual gathering *symbel*.

Using the evidence of Old English texts - mainly the epic *Beowulf* and the *Anglo-Saxon Chronicles*, Stephen Pollington shows that the idea of feasting remained central to early English social traditions long after the physical reality had declined in importance.

The words of the poets and saga-writers are supported by a wealth of archaeological data dealing with halls, settlement layouts and magnificent feasting gear found in many early Anglo-Saxon graves.

Three appendices cover:
- Hall-themes in Old English verse;
- Old English and translated texts;
- The structure and origins of the warband.

£14.95   ISBN 1-898281-30-0   9 ¾ x 6 ¾ inches   248 x 170mm   hardback   288 pages

Tastes of Anglo-Saxon England
Mary Savelli

These easy to follow recipes will enable you to enjoy a mix of ingredients and flavours that were widely known in Anglo-Saxon England but are rarely experienced today. In addition to the 46 recipes, there is background information about households and cooking techniques.

£4.95   ISBN 1-898281-28-9   A5   80 pages

English Sea Power 871-1100 AD
John Pullen-Appleby

This work examines the largely untold story of English sea power during the period 871 to 1100. It was an age when English kings deployed warships first against Scandinavian invaders and later in support of Continental allies.

The author has gathered together information about the appearance of warships and how they were financed, crewed, and deployed.

Price £14.95   144 pages   hardcover   ISBN 1-898281-31-9

Latest Titles

Anglo-Saxon Attitudes – A short introduction to Anglo-Saxonism
J.A. Hilton

This is not a book about the Anglo-Saxons, but a book about books about Anglo-Saxons. It describes the academic discipline of Anglo-Saxonism; the methods of study used; the underlying assumptions; and the uses to which it has been put.

Methods and motives have changed over time but right from the start there have been constant themes: English patriotism and English freedom.

£6.95   A5   ISBN 1–898281–39-4   Hardback 64pp

The Origins of the Anglo-Saxons
Donald Henson

This book has come about through a growing frustration with scholarly analysis and debate about the beginnings of Anglo-Saxon England. Much of what has been written is excellent, yet unsatisfactory. One reason for this is that scholars often have only a vague acquaintance with fields outside their own specialism. The result is a partial examination of the evidence and an incomplete understanding or explanation of the period.

The growth and increasing dominance of archaeological evidence for the period has been accompanied by an unhealthy enthusiasm for models of social change imported from prehistory. Put simply, many archaeologists have developed a complete unwillingness to consider movements of population as a factor in social, economic or political change. All change becomes a result of indigenous development, and all historically recorded migrations become merely the movement of a few hundred aristocrats or soldiers. The author does not find this credible.

£19.95   A5   ISBN 1–898281–40-2   304pp

A Departed Music – Readings in Old English Poetry
Walter Nash

The *readings* of this book take the form of passages of translation from some Old English poems. The author paraphrases their content and discuses their place and significance in the history of poetic art in Old English society and culture.

The authors knowledge, enthusiasm and love of his subject help make this an excellent introduction to the subject for students and the general reader.

£16.95   A5   ISBN 1–898281–37-8   240pp

Rudiments of Runelore
Stephen Pollington

The purpose of this book is to provide both a comprehensive introduction for those coming to the subject for the first time, and a handy and inexpensive reference work for those with some knowledge of the subject. The *Abecedarium Nordmannicum* and the English, Norwegian and Icelandic rune poems are included as are two rune riddles, extracts from the Cynewulf poems and new work on the three Brandon runic inscriptions and the Norfolk 'Tiw' runes.

Headings include: The Origin of the Runes; Runes among the Germans; The Germanic Rune Row and the Common Germanic Language; The English Runic Tradition; The Scandinavian Runic Tradition; Runes and Pseudo-runes; The Use of Runes; Bind Runes and Runic Cryptography.

£4.95   ISBN 1–898281–16–5   A5   Illustrations   96 pages

Rune Cards
Brian Partridge & Tony Linsell

"This boxed set of 30 cards contains some of the most beautiful and descriptive black and white line drawings that I have ever seen on this subject."

Pagan News

30 pen and ink drawings by Brian Partridge
80 page booklet by Tony Linsell gives information about the origin of runes, their meaning, and how to read them.

£9.95   ISBN 1-898281-34-3   30 cards & 80 page booklet – boxed

English Sea Power 871-1100AD
John Pullen-Appleby

This work examines the largely untold story of English sea power prior to the Norman Conquest. The author illuminates the much-neglected period 871 to 1100, an age when English rulers deployed naval resources, first against Norse Invaders, and later as an instrument of state in relations with neighbouring countries.

The author has gathered together information about the crewing, appearance and use of fighting ships during the period.

£14.95   ISBN 1-898281-31-9   9 ¾ x 6 ¾ inches   245 x 170mm   128 pages

Ordering
Payment may be made by Visa, or Mastercard. Telephone orders accepted.
See website for postal address
UK deliveries add 10% up to a maximum of £2-50
Europe – including **Republic of Ireland** - add 10% plus £1 – all orders sent airmail
North America add 10% surface delivery, 30% airmail
Elsewhere add 10% surface delivery, 40% airmail
Overseas surface delivery 5–8 weeks; airmail 5–10 days
For details of other titles and our North American distributor see our website or contact us at:

Anglo-Saxon Books
web site: www.asbooks.co.uk   e-mail: enq@asbooks.co.uk
Tel: 0845 430 4200   Fax: 0845 430 4201

Organisations

Þa Engliscan Gesiðas

Þa Engliscan Gesiðas (The English Companions) is a historical and cultural society exclusively devoted to Anglo-Saxon history. Its aims are to bridge the gap between scholars and non-experts, and to bring together all those with an interest in the Anglo-Saxon period, its language, culture and traditions, so as to promote a wider interest in, and knowledge of all things Anglo-Saxon. The Fellowship publishes a journal, *Wiðowinde,* which helps members to keep in touch with current thinking on topics from art and archaeology to heathenism and Early English Christianity. The Fellowship enables like-minded people to keep in contact by publicising conferences, courses and meetings that might be of interest to its members.

For further details see www.kami.demon.co.uk/gesithas/ or write to: The Membership Secretary, Þa Engliscan Gesiðas, BM Box 4336, London, WC1N 3XX England.

Regia Anglorum

Regia Anglorum was founded to accurately re-create the life of the British people as it was around the time of the Norman Conquest. Our work has a strong educational slant. We consider authenticity to be of prime importance and prefer, where possible, to work from archaeological materials. Approximately twenty-five per cent of our members, of over 500 people, are archaeologists or historians.

The Society has a large working Living History Exhibit, teaching and exhibiting more than twenty crafts in an authentic environment. We own a forty-foot wooden ship replica of a type that would have been a common sight in Northern European waters around the turn of the first millennium AD. Battle re-enactment is another aspect of our activities, often involving 200 or more warriors.

For further information see www.regia.org or contact: K. J. Siddorn, 9 Durleigh Close, Headley Park, Bristol BS13 7NQ, England, e-mail: kim_siddorn@compuserve.com

The Sutton Hoo Society

Our aims and objectives focus on promoting research and education relating to the Anglo Saxon Royal cemetery at Sutton Hoo, Suffolk in the UK. The Society publishes a newsletter SAXON twice a year, which keeps members up to date with society activities, carries resumes of lectures and visits, and reports progress on research and publication associated with the site. If you would like information about membership see website: www.suttonhoo.org

Wuffing Education

Wuffing Education provides those interested in the history, archaeology, literature and culture of the Anglo-Saxons with the chance to meet experts and fellow enthusiasts for a whole day of in-depth seminars and discussions. Day Schools take place at the historic Tranmer House overlooking the burial mounds of Sutton Hoo in Suffolk.

For details of programme of events contact:-
Wuffing Education, 4 Hilly Fields, Woodbridge, Suffolk IP12 4DX
email education@wuffings.co.uk   website www.wuffings.co.uk
Tel. 01394 383908 or 01728 688749

Places to visit

Bede's World at Jarrow

Bede's world tells the remarkable story of the life and times of the Venerable Bede, 673–735 AD. Visitors can explore the origins of early medieval Northumbria and Bede's life and achievements through his own writings and the excavations of the monasteries at Jarrow and other sites.

Location – 10 miles from Newcastle upon Tyne, off the A19 near the southern entrance to the River Tyne tunnel. Bus services 526 & 527

Bede's World, Church Bank, Jarrow, Tyne and Wear, NE32 3DY
Tel. 0191 489 2106; Fax: 0191 428 2361; website: www.bedesworld.co.uk

Sutton Hoo near Woodbridge, Suffolk

Sutton Hoo is a group of low burial mounds overlooking the River Deben in south-east Suffolk. Excavations in 1939 brought to light the richest burial ever discovered in Britain – an Anglo-Saxon ship containing a magnificent treasure which has become one of the principal attractions of the British Museum. The mound from which the treasure was dug is thought to be the grave of Rædwald, an early English king who died in 624/5 AD.

This National Trust site has an excellent visitor centre, which includes a reconstruction of the burial chamber and its grave goods. Some original objects as well as replicas of the treasure are on display.

2 miles east of Woodbridge on B1083   Tel. 01394 389700

West Stow Anglo-Saxon Village

An early Anglo-Saxon Settlement reconstructed on the site where it was excavated consisting of timber and thatch hall, houses and workshop. There is also a museum containing objects found during the excavation of the site. Open all year 10am–4.15pm (except Yuletide). Special provision for school parties. A teachers' resource pack is available. Costumed events are held on some weekends, especially Easter Sunday and August Bank Holiday Monday. Craft courses are organised.

For further details see www.stedmunds.co.uk/west_stow.html or contact:
The Visitor Centre, West Stow Country Park, Icklingham Road, West Stow,
Bury St Edmunds, Suffolk IP28 6HG   Tel. 01284 728718